What do I do now, Lord?

By Jeanette Struchen

What do I do now, Lord?

JEANETTE STRUCHEN

FLEMING H. REVELL COMPANY

OLD TAPPAN, NEW JERSEY

FOR
Phyllis and Jared

Introduction

For some women the middle years are about as necessary as being overstocked on olives. These years create an epidemic of restlessness, a chronic decentralization of faith, and vague fears that life is evaporating. It's like banging our heads in the dark unable to find a light as anxiety and tension create irreverent rebellion.

Whatever our reaction, it is a time when all our resources are called up for active service. There may be a few women whose days are spent calmly cutting roses in the garden but most of us spend a lot of time in crash helmets adjusting our shock absorbers.

Problems, decisions, crises, and hang-ups come in every size from mini to maxi and our reactions are as varied. For instance we may:

> ruffle our feathers
> put up guard rails
> build an inside maze
> storm the bastions
> run a bucket of tears
> hope for clairvoyance
> give up
> study alternatives
> pray for guidance

consult a pro
expect a miracle

We may do all, some, or none of these but above everything else it's necessary to hang in there and face each installment of life as it comes.

Sometimes our best contribution may be to do nothing. Sometimes our best may be to give nonverbal support to a pattern of action. Sometimes it may be to pick up the problem and carry it full weight, piggyback.

The middle of life is a time for signal watching—careful signal watching—for readiness to put on the brakes, for necessity to call up more power, for emergency to come to a screeching halt, or for opportunity to become a lighthouse.

These pages concern themselves with signals during the middle years at crossroads where circumstances meet decisions and decisions meet responses. Thankfully, no one of us has been confronted with every account, but the following represent true experiences poured out to the Almighty and later shared with me during my own middle years while leading retreats, teaching school, and being a preacher's wife.

JEANETTE STRUCHEN

*I'm not a radical but I do think the kids
have a point. Most adults are idol happy.
We worship a lot of hand-me-down ideas and
long-range promises expecting our kids to do
the same.*

I STARED AGHAST, LORD. I COULDN'T BELIEVE MY
ears. This from my fifty-year-old friend who collects antiques
and usually thinks as square as dice.

We live in a college town where there have been pickets for
twenty-five years. The first pickets I ever saw walked with
signs in front of campus barber shops. Since then, we have
had demonstrations, tear gas, moratoriums, and militia. Most
of us have nailed our doors shut and pulled the plug on anything piped in from the college.

"Your taxes paid for those burned buildings. Now do you
think the kids are right?"

"Whoa! Did I say they were right to burn the buildings?"

"You said the kids have a point."

"Back up. We're not communicating. What I said was the
kids have a point in wanting to think for themselves and not
idolize all the ideas we've spoon fed them. I said nothing
about burning buildings. You did."

"The two go together. How can you separate their radical
thinking from their radical behavior?"

"What's radical? My mother was a radical when she bobbed
her hair and my grandmother was a radical because she
wouldn't ride sidesaddle. Labels come unglued with time.

9

To me, burning down public property is a criminal act. I expect it to be treated as such by authorities even though the kids used it as shock treatment for the community. Frustration and exasperation breed hot-tempered action."

"Kids never had it as good as they have it today—beautiful campus, elegant dorms, endless opportunities. Why shake it up?"

"Because they see social inconsistencies, inequalities, weaknesses which could be cured but aren't. They see great sums of money being used irresponsibly. They hear our adage about peace on earth but don't see us working for it. They smell graft in high places and feel society's pressure to grab instead of give."

"You're a hippie—an honest to goodness hippie." I said.

"They wouldn't have me," she laughed. "I'm too old. But as I said they do have a point. Most of us adults are over-impressed with what we have rather than what we are and we are more apt to glorify the past, stubbornly whitewashing our mistakes rather than admit to them and learn from them."

"Who would have thought it? You're a hippie."

"Stop labeling and start listening. You're so busy sticking me in a mold you can't hear what I'm saying."

Maybe I was and maybe she is right, Lord, but suddenly she is a problem to me. I have a whole list of controversial subjects to avoid when talking with her. I don't want to get her started again because she shakes me up.

You've got to be kidding. With grades like mine you expect me to go to college? Let's face it I'm a dud.
Face it is what I'm trying to do. Today you can't get anyplace without college.
But I don't want to get anyplace, Mother. Let me be me.

LORD, YOU REMEMBER HOW BLITHELY I CALLED IT only her growing-up process. I felt she owed her parents something. She felt we were obligated to her as parents. I felt she needed our help. She felt we were imposing on her right to make decisions. I thought I was challenging her to success in life. She was daring us with her ability to fail.

I was too proud to talk it out with someone who works with teen-agers because it meant admitting defeat. This was a mistake Lord. I know it now. Much of the impasse was caused by my inability to recognize that many teen-agers feel this way. The situation was not unique. To know it earlier would have saved a lot of guilty self-whipping.

Thanks for guiding us to stand back and take another look. From studying seriously the pattern on grade cards I learned that what we interpreted as causes for poor grades (too much TV, time on the telephone, wasting time) were actually her intellectual inability to perform at our expectation level. Not all the study rules, bribes, and grounding on weekends could affect that. (We may have known this unconsciously but couldn't face it consciously.) Naturally, this kept her motivation low because she knew she couldn't win on our expectation level. Therefore, she didn't even want to compete.

Lord, looking back on it I remember we kept on bribing her with clothes and gadgets.

What happened?

Nothing very big. Except as a mother I am learning to accept that she is not moving backward and that I am not a failure because she doesn't want to go to college. You and I both know, Lord, that she is the same girl only happier because I am reading her as she is and not what I expect her to be.

Do you hear me?
No, I'm not listening.

HE WASN'T LISTENING, LORD, BECAUSE HE DIDN'T WANT
to. He couldn't hear me because the stereo was high enough
to make the windows rattle.

It was low tide, wasn't it, Lord, when Rob came home at
the end of his freshman year at college with wedding bells in
his ears?

You know, Lord, we were not against their marriage. We
were against it at that point in life. Education was expensive
enough without taking on a wife. Any ordinary setback—
baby, rent, outside jobs—would take away study time toward
career preparation and nobody becomes a mechanical engineer
in a day or gets very far without a college degree.

"But I love her," he kept saying.

We answered, "Real love waits."

"But maybe the army will snag me and hoist me off to war."

We answered, "Real love waits."

"But she gives me incentive to study. We're both good students."

We answered, "A career should offer incentive, too."

"We're together all the time anyway. The college has open
dorm rules."

We answered, "Well, we hope you have more sense than to
take advantage of that."

Remember, Lord, how we went around and around? I

knew college had changed, but Rob's entire thought pattern had changed in nine college months. He argued about the stupidities of academic policies, advocated free love, mixed marriage, and revolution. His parental insensitivity was unbelievable. He was irritable all day and restless all night. He had no loyalty to the college and even expostulated against the church. There was no end to it.

Lord, at first we thought it was a phase. Remember? Then we knew better.

Our attempts at solution began by inviting his girl to visit. She came. We liked Ginny, thought her immature, but we weren't marrying her.

Over the dinner table the two spoke freely of their friends who had run away for the summer to be together. Some went into communes and others to cheap rooms to live together. They talked about a lot of dorm activity which twenty years ago would have brought college expulsion.

Then, O God, remember how we began to count our blessings? Rob had asked us about marriage. He had not lived with her as a runaway for the summer. We met her. He did not bring her home and say, "Guess who's coming to dinner?" He loves her and she loves him. They didn't come in saying she was pregnant.

After considering our blessings, we consented to the marriage. Now, Lord, we're standing by to help if invited to do so.

WANTED:
Experienced secretary
Good working conditions
Hours: 9 to 5; 5-day week
Salary attractive
Reply - Box 743

Should I go back to work? Why, Lord, is it so hard to make a decision?

MY REASONING TOLD ME, GO!

Financially, we had a few debts. George was at the final level on the office salary scale and the twins were starting college in another year. College expenses were covered but barely. This might plug the profit drain.

Psychologically, it would help me over the lonely hump of getting up to a vacant house when the twins leave.

Socially, it would give me new outlets for friends.

Mentally, if the job was right, it would help keep me alert. The neighbor to neighbor coffee klatch isn't my thing.

Remember, Lord, how I decided that the greatest detriment was being tied up in the summer and during winter breaks when the twins would be home? Also, work would keep me from accompanying George on business trips. These weren't regular but they were fun.

Thank you for helping me realize that time alone doesn't work out decisions. I had to take the first step. Regularly, I glanced over the ads to get a picture of opportunities. Then

I sifted them by interest, location, and time involved (full- or part-time). I decided on part-time.

I started asking acquaintances about part-time work—the receptionist in our doctor's office, the librarian, and the court house clerk. I realized part-time workers get few advantages, erratic hours, often unimaginative work, and little flexibility on privileges.

Once I went for an interview but they wanted a student-age person.

Another time I was required to sign up for several courses which I didn't want to do.

The outcome was funny, wasn't it, Lord?

After careful thought I couldn't bring myself to apply anywhere at all. The closer I got the more apprehensive I became.

Finally, I realized that what looked good was the extra money in the family till and what I really wanted was freedom.

Recently, at the suggestion of a neighbor (maybe it was Your idea, Lord), I signed up to be a hospital volunteer two days a week—distributing mail, wheeling patients to X-ray, and delivering plants. I'm needed. It's just what I wanted. Yes, it's just exactly what I wanted.

*I gave $100 to help refurnish those rooms
and now slum kids are romping all over the
place.*

LORD, I WAS ONLY TRYING TO HELP.

It started with an all-out campaign to help our youth at the
church. We raised $2500 to redecorate the downstairs with
bright furniture and a soft-drink bar. Without children of
my own, I enjoyed helping and some of us spent hours painting walls so younger painters could add designs. It was fun
and I was sorry when it ended.

Now, Lord, the rooms are being used daily for all the preschool kids in the church neighborhood. They race through
the halls and roll all over new carpets.

I had several phone calls from people who were as upset as
I. Finally, I called the president of our Women's Guild.

"Is it necessary to have our property used like this?" I
asked.

"We've started a preschool program. The church yard is
used for games and the rooms for an educational program to
give kids a jump on first grade."

"That's not the job of the church, is it?" I asked.

"Then what is the job of the church?"

"Well," I stammered, "it's to teach us to be better Christians
and give us a place to worship. I feel it is to serve those who
belong here and we, in turn, send money to help the needy."

"You are right, of course. Helping the needy is the whole
point. Sometimes the needy is us. Sometimes it's half a world

17

away. Sometimes it's on our doorstep. Our church is set down in a neighborhood of need."

"Guess my idea of need is different from yours. I think of needy people as those without food and clothing."

"You're right. Need can be physical. It can also be psychological, spiritual, and even educational. Don't you agree?"

"Yes, but those rooms were meant for our youth," I said.

"It's our youth who are sponsoring the preschool program. They initiated it. They lead games, tell stories, and bring guitars for singing. More than that, each of our young people is assigned to one neighborhood child and they talk, learn new ideas, and listen to each other. They call it a one to one teach-in. This program is a whole mission thing but our youth haven't realized that yet. After all isn't this what the missionary idea of the church is all about?"

Lord, her question puzzled me. My idea of mission isn't exactly that but I stifled my urge to say so. It seems to me the Office of Public Instruction or Public Welfare should be supporting a preschool program if there is need. I can't see that the church should saddle itself with it. The way I see it, the whole neighborhood is full of irresponsible people on welfare who shouldn't be having kids if they can't take care of them.

One of these days I'll take up the invitation to see the preschool in action, but it may be a long time, Lord, before I see anything down there but rooms being abused.

His temperature went to 106°. The only thing to do was pray.

O GOD, REMEMBER HOW I PRAYED FOR A MIRACLE— sudden and complete? There was no time for long-range hope amid the shrinking rumor that Billy could get well.

My mind kept the prayer going without words, Lord. Every passing hour he lived was an oasis where I could breathe deeply and allow myself the reward of hope.

Nurses tiptoed in and out of his room never looking my way. I walked the hall within sight of Billy's door. Hours passed and between clock watching and door watching I began to think more clearly about my prayer.

Healing, I decided, is accomplished by doctors, nurses, medicine, time, and the body working within Your plan of healing.

Illness I decided, is out of character with the plan of Your goodness. So I began to pray for the doctors and nurses who administered the medicine at appropriate times to bring about Your plan for healing. I prayed for the slightest details contributing to Billy's welfare.

Hours passed. Sometimes ten minutes were longer than an hour. Prayers flashed through my mind.

Suddenly it came to mind that the ultimate prayer was "Thy will be done." The idea repelled me because I rejected the danger implied that whatever happened to Billy would be acceptable because it was Your will. I couldn't pray it. It was a gamble I couldn't risk.

19

During the night, Lord, Billy died and tenderly I bundled the long night watch and tucked it in my heart where every detail is alive. Never was I strong enough to pray "Thy will be done" but I leaned on it, Lord or I would have disintegrated in grief.

Quiet everybody. Mother is about to point out AGAIN where she went to school.

AS WE DROVE BY I DIDN'T LAUGH WITH THE REST OF the family but I felt, Lord, that they had an organized secret about me. They knew me better than I knew myself. I was predictable.

At first it made me so angry I considered joining a trapeze act just to show them!

Then I considered it was I who needed jolting. Maybe a short course or part-time job would do it.

Lastly, I considered that maybe they liked me predictable. They could count on me—knew where I stood on things—and there were, after all, worse things than being predictable. They could count on me, Lord.

My mother will be here. Just hand it to her at the door.

Come on over anytime. My wife is always around. She'll be glad to have company 'til I get home.

We'll keep your cat when you're away. My mother is always home.

Such statements made me sound like a stay-at-home while everybody else was out and doing. But You know I'm happy at home. It's where I want to be. After all, not every woman needs to be on a committee or golf course or in an office. I'd rather raise African violets.

21

Maybe it's malignant.
The words triggered a thousand deaths.

NOBODY KNOWS UNTIL SHE'S BEEN THROUGH IT, LORD, but everyone frames a mental picture of what it's like to come full face with the possibility of cancer. We imagine the initial shock and every unfolding stage. It becomes a tattoo on the mind.

Unanswerable questions spill out. How much chance? Shall I tell the family? Do I really want to know the whole truth? What has to be done to me? How soon? How sure is the doctor?

In waiting rooms I heard things like:

Fearfully, I was riding the coattails of a comet—unpredictable and spinning all the way.

Nobody could convince me otherwise. I was sure it was cancer—knew it all the time.

The very mountains shook in disbelief. It couldn't happen to me.

Courage is not my dish.

Doctor, what should I do now?

How much I learned, Lord. First, I learned that the doctor has an answer in terms of physical treatment. Spiritual treatment was up to me. Then, I learned that fear is not illusion.

It creates an illness all its own and can prevent healing as surely as courage and faith can invite it. Fear kicked down my nerve and weakened my fighting capacity. Fear slammed the door on courage and left me walking the gauntlet alone.

Later, I learned that mustering courage during illness is easier than it sounds. It simply appeared out of intense need. I found a supply beyond that which I thought I had.

Most important of all (even beyond family loyalty and my fumbling prayer life) was the discovery of a core of inner quietness where I was at peace. It was a spot where I had a sense of wholeness about the meaning of life and death. In fact it was the only spot, Lord, where I wasn't fragmented. I found it when I accepted the fact that whether I lived or died I was held in Your Everlasting Arms. It was as simple as that.

*My son is a twenty-four-year-old drug addict.
He started sniffing glue, went on to pot and
became psychologically addicted to it. By
sixteen he was mainlining heroin. At seven-
teen he was picked up on breaking and
entering to support his expensive habit.*

WASN'T I NAÏVE ABOUT DRUGS, LORD? AND WASN'T
Bob cagey beyond belief? I went through his closet and found
hidden a small set of gadgets which I didn't even recognize as
instruments for cooking and shooting drugs into his veins.
I learned fast.

O God, what do I do now? I asked it over and over.

I was shocked, frightened, furious, and guilty in that order.
My husband and I spent hours asking, Why?

We knew nothing about drugs, not even their names. Our
appalling ignorance was a part of the problem for which there
is no one-way solution. It was a sin, Lord, to be so totally
irrelevant to a major issue in contemporary life, thinking drugs
were for kids in ghettos. Our beautiful suburban home was
hardly the setting, was it?

Remember the day in the presence of police, Lord, when for
the first time we confronted Bob? The issue at hand was
larceny, not drugs. He was caught with $123.63 taken from a
grocery. Only after long persistent questioning did he con-
fess drug use although all along it had been the police sus-
picion. All the time we thought he wanted the money toward
a car.

25

He has had jail, bail, and treatment at a residential drug center. He hasn't learned much. One of the most important things we have learned has been that drug users are chronic liars. It is totally unbelievable how sincere they can be in the middle of lies.

Then it ended, Lord, when I overheard the makings of a party. There were names of people I had never heard of. Party night came and for once, at least, we knew where he was. We discussed whether to call the police. Calling would result in many arrests, including our son's. We called. Police raided the party. Arrests were made and a discovered drug cache was sizable. Bob was back in jail.

You know, Lord, I have cried a river, self-whipped, and pleaded to You for help. I have also studied our drug laws, visited lawmakers, and learned a lot about police, judges, and jails.

I have joined a county-wide group for parents of addicts who speak, upon invitation, to any organization in the area to alert parents to the drug scene. We plan to lobby for tougher laws not looser ones.

Beyond this I don't know what to do. My son is in another center starting methadone treatment. We'll see, Lord. We'll have to wait and see.

I'm about to short circuit myself.

I KEEP THINKING ABOUT HER, LORD, BUT DON'T EVEN remember her name. She was pretty, bright, and fun. Her contribution to the retreat had been exceptional. Not only had she served on the steering committee but before coming she had organized a family of four back home.

In group discussion her questions were prodding, her answers thoughtful. People listened when she spoke. She was never pushy.

She was on every committee not only at Sunday school and church but also in the PTA and Cub Scouts. But her looks, personality, and wit were working to her detriment. She had juggled activities, declined new jobs, then out of guilt accepted. She took on jobs where little was expected but she turned each into a crusade.

Quiet time alone was nonexistent. Her reading time was long gone. Relaxation made her feel guilty. She was overextended physically, mentally, and spiritually and knew it. Knowing it was half the solution.

Near the end of the retreat she announced a big, personal decision. She was declaring a sabbatical year from outside activities. It was to be her year and it began with *no.* To outsiders it sounded selfish but she knew You would understand and it was the beginning of the campaign to glue herself together.

27

*How can you say that? I'm only trying to
help.
But your help is more than I need. I need
time to space out on my own. Moving to an
apartment has nothing to do with whether I
love you, Mother. It has everything to do
with whether I can handle myself without
leaning and without waiting for your daily
instructions.*

INTELLECTUALLY SHE WAS MATURE. WASN'T SHE,
Lord? She had proved it. But emotionally I felt she needed
a rescue squad. To cut loose the moorings was a gamble I
finally agreed with reluctance. Remember, Lord, how I
wrestled with that decision?

Her job paid well and a promotion came out of competency.
We suggested she not sign a two-year apartment lease but our
advice was covered by her excitement over new furniture and
painting parties.

Within six months she quit her job. Her employer couldn't
explain. Neither could we. When asked, the answer was
that she wanted to hang loose for awhile.

"What about the apartment?"

"Who cares! They can't do any more than throw me out
and you and Dad wouldn't let that happen."

For the first time ever, Lord, I saw us as her rescue squad.
She expected it. My husband and I spent hours reviewing all

29

the times we had come to her rescue feeling it was a parental duty. We were her insurance against disaster.

Mentally, we rehearsed excuses for her to our friends and neighbors. One day we heard ourselves defending her behavior to each other. At that moment, Lord, we dropped our defenses, swallowed parental pride, and faced the truth. We stopped rescuing her. Do You remember how shaky I was through all this?

The landlord evicted her and kept the furniture.

She was shocked and heartbroken but we stood mute. She disappeared. We were frantic but did not look for her. After five days she came home like the Prodigal to an all-round reunion of tears and new resolutions. She wanted to move in to stay. We allowed her to stay for one month until she found a job and another apartment. This was agreeable. The time limit let her know we believed in her sense of responsibility to get a job, to pay the rent, and shift for herself. By the end of the month she had a temporary job and a poorly furnished room. We said nothing.

We learned through the experience that always we had been too eager to help, to shield, and to rescue. Overprotection is often mistaken as mother love.

She learned that what she thought she didn't need (our help) she was completely dependent upon. How true this is when we try to go it alone without You, Lord!

Mom, I've had it with church. Those people are a buncha hypocrites proppin' each other up. Sunday morning is a drag.

AT SIX HE WOULD NOT SAY A WORD. AT SIXTEEN HE was a verbal superrigged bulldozer.

Lord, I had been expecting his outburst. For months we had urged Jack's church attendance on the basis of family loyalty. Pressure solved nothing. Now we had no alternative but to allow him freedom to discover the church in his own way, in his own time, on his own terms. We knew, Lord, his personal discovery might never come.

On Sunday mornings Jack listened to records or slept. He seldom had recreational plans until after we were home from church. Casually, we continued to talk about church activities, the sermon, and who was present. He entered in with questions and comments.

"Of course, they're hypocrites," my husband said. "Aren't we all? Nobody ever said the church was made up of saints."

"They're tryin' to act like it."

"Yes, they are. That's the whole point. The church is a buncha people, as you say, who are hypocrites and sinners. They know it—admit it—and they're trying to improve."

"Well, they act like they're perfect and setting themselves up as examples of perfection to the community."

We let the subject drop.

Once the sermon was entitled "What Are You Celebrating?" The preacher said worship has to be a celebration of joy that

31

You exist, Lord, that You care for us, that You should be a great event in our lives, and that every day should be a cause for celebration.

"Then after all that talk about celebrating he announced some drab hymn," Jack said.

"No, he lit a lot of candles as symbols of our celebration. He also mentioned that it's no fun to celebrate alone. Nobody likes to celebrate alone on birthdays or Christmas and if we're celebrating something on Sunday it's great to do it with our friends," my husband explained.

No comment.

Another time the subject of the preacher came up.

"He's no saint," Jack said.

"No, he's not. But he's an honest guy who sees people as they are and he believes in them. He doesn't have all the answers and says so, but he sees the mixed-up mess in the world as the rest of us do only he hasn't lost hope, and that's quite a feat."

No comment.

Lord, we are not pushing. Maybe we should. At this point we know only that our communication line is still intact and for that much we are thankful.

Whatever happened to salvation of souls? All I hear about now is the church's involvement in social action. Chalk it up to anything you want but I say we're surrendering to alternatives in the church. Salvation of souls is what it's all about and anything less is playing hooky from the job.

LORD, ONLY YOU KNOW HOW THIS WORRIES ME. MY conservative background is rich and strong. I still enjoy the old songs and a rousing preacher who calls me sinner, then tells me to repent. The whole process of being saved is a beautiful experience of Your love for man and man's ability to shake loose his rebelliousness by surrendering to a better way. Yet, I keep replaying that talk I had with my friend.

"You've got the whole idea in a nutshell, Judy," Carol said, "and the idea never changes—only the techniques."

"What do you mean?"

"I don't know what I mean except that you're saying God hopes man will learn to behave himself and man is forever in there punching to be free and easy. The church is in there trying to get them together. When one technique doesn't work the church tries another."

"Sounds too easy the way you explain it."

"Okay, make it complicated. Let's go shopping."

"I don't want to make it complicated. I want to make it meaningful."

"It is meaningful. I don't mean to be flippant but remember your emotions are involved here. When you talk about your beautiful experience of salvation, can't it be just as

33

beautiful when it happens through a love experience or discovery or joy or wonder or a job or learning to read or helping somebody or . . ."

"Okay I get the point. You're saying the experience of being saved from the old is only half the problem. That becoming new is the rest of it."

"Something like that."

"Well, how does that happen?"

"Are you sure you want all this? For me, first, I believe God allows it to happen. Not by pulling strings to have us in the right spot at the right time but by creating conditions whereby we can change our minds, adapt to the new, get motivated to do something and be something. All these possibilities are given to us. They are inherent.

"Next, I believe we have a better chance for all this if we are healthy, have a decent place to live, and some pride in being a human being. Not everybody has this. Some people live in rattraps, eat garbage, and see themselves as the dumping ground of society. How can people like that think about your beautiful salvation when they're a jungle of social problems?"

"You mean only people without problems can be saved?"

"No, I mean people can't think about their souls when other things are squeezing the life out of them. The church recognizes this and by being involved in social problems it is helping people to fulfill God's intention for them."

"But the whole New Testament is about salvation."

"Sure it is but it doesn't say anywhere that there's only one route to it. Some people had to be fed before they listened, some changed jobs to follow Jesus, and one had to wash his eyes so he could see better."

"Are you saying I've been blind and ought to wash my eyes?"

"No, I'm saying let's wash our coffee cups and go shopping."

Lord, something tells me that this conversation was important. Maybe I'll never believe as Carol but if nothing else our talk makes me feel closer to her.

Think young? I'm trying.

LORD, THE PAST TEN YEARS HAVE BEEN NOTHING BUT static so I'm using a rear-view mirror to look back at the earlier years.

Aging throws a special glow over the years when nothing seemed to be happening except growing up. Those years slipped under my belt unnoticed. But maybe I am, in great degree, what those quiet green years made me.

I'm talking, Lord, about the process of becoming what I became—days when I dreamed big over ice cream, wished on stars, crossed my heart, and had energy coming out my ears.

I'm a complicated mosaic. I feel like a part of everybody I ever met, every book I ever read, and every experience I ever had. That's me—bits and pieces shaped by many people and glued together by You.

Maybe this is a middle-aged game of tiddly-winks, Lord, when I'm trying to snap everything into a neat little cup and when every piece is in place I've won. But what have I won?

There are days when I think the greatest prize of all was having You and time on my side.

There's no other way. Mother must come to
live with us.
His words came loud and clear.

AT FIRST I THOUGHT I WOULD NEED A RABBIT'S FOOT
and crystal ball to deal with her under our roof. Then, Lord,
I decided a dab of intelligence and a lot of prayer would do it.

Worrying about it wouldn't help. Over the years I had
said it to everybody in the family. They quoted it back when
my husband pronounced the ultimatum.

Lord, did You ever know a part-time invalid (and increasingly cranky) who ruled an entire nursing home by cane and
bell? She built up steam over nothing and exploded frequently. Her worst moments seemed to be during visiting
hours. Either she was showing the family how well she had
things under control or showing the nurses she had a family
behind her. No one had illusions, Lord, about her need for
a personality transplant.

Physically, arrangements were easy. We had a room on the
first floor which could be converted for her.

Mentally, the family had a lot of preparation. Remember,
Lord, how we balked? At my husband's wise request we held
several discussions where he alone turned the tide saying, with
apology, that there was no other way than to bring Grandma
into our home. Money for nursing homes had simply run out.
He admitted she was difficult and temperamental. Beyond
that he knew she was miserable in every way. He gave us
alternatives.

Either we could create an unlivable situation for all of us by keeping her miserable or by concentrated effort we could be kind, hoping she would catch it. With Your help, Lord, we caught his idea.

On moving day our two teen-agers put a welcome sign over the front door and flowers in her room. From the first day we gave her little jobs to do so she wouldn't feel in the way. Sometimes they had to be created on the spur of the moment but she felt needed.

Often we invited over her old friends and we cleared out to give them privacy.

There were explosions. O Lord, do You recall how for days we would tiptoe around those subjects which raised her to boiling point? Hardest of all was giving in to her TV shows. Sometimes she threatened to move out. Other times we threatened to move her out. Once in awhile all of us sat around the table, smoked a peace pipe, and started over.

It worked, Lord. Kindness rubbed off and was repaid with kindness. When our supply ran short, we pumped it up and crossed our fingers.

Grandma has been dead for two years now. God bless her soul. Her empty room is still Grandma's room. Her presence created a bridge of gaps but it also created a beautifully carved family allegiance, which followed her all the way to the grave.

Afraid of death?

NO, I'M NOT, LORD. THAT'S NOT MY PROBLEM.

If You knew enough to make a world reusing the least atom You have sense enough to reuse Your peak of creation, which is man. Wastefulness doesn't seem to be a part of Your nature.

Granted there are days when I advise You to start over with the atoms.

There's nothing wrong with collecting antiques but I don't want to be one.

I AM A SQUIRREL AND SAVE EVERYTHING FROM OLD hatpins to valentines. Lord, You know I am sentimental by nature. I enjoy the old and my family jokes about it but threatens to drop a match in the attic.

Our closets are full of boxes inside boxes inside other boxes. Funny, isn't it, Lord, how some people save everything. Maybe it's a sin. Each box holds precious items—pictures of family two and three generations back, postcards collected on summer vacations when I was a girl, old jewelry, cloth from my grandmother's dress, scrapbooks, and parts of beloved toys.

I have our old ice-cream mixer, old tax receipts, and surveying records. There is a box of old sheet music collected during early years of marriage and handmade doll clothes. There is a box of buttons and the purchase papers of a long-gone pony.

Lord, my first conclusion on this problem is that sorting takes discipline which I don't have. Some women sort easily. I don't. Maybe it's a problem of my inability to make decisions. Some women had parents who made decisions for them. Others married a strong spouse. Some had permissive parents who encouraged collections and later had husbands who gently tolerated them. My family tolerates them on the surface but secretly debunks it underneath. They say jokingly that I collect Early Miscellaneous.

Lord, my second conclusion on this problem is that I am the

41

kind of woman who does not live in the present only but in insatiable fantasies of days never again to be.

My final conclusion is that it's time to telephone an antique dealer and then a secondhand dealer. In that order. I hear, Lord, that cash encourages sorting.

*Your Honor, we, the jury, find the defendant
guilty as charged.
The foreman's words were the beginning of
five years imprisonment.*

MY HUSBAND IS AN EX-CONVICT TRYING TO MAKE IT
back into society. Lord, aren't people ever going to forgive?
Everywhere he turns doors are shut. A barber by training, his
prison record keeps him from obtaining a state barber's
license, and if he can't get an acceptable job I'm afraid he will
get an unacceptable one. In order to get any job at all he
seems to have to lie about his background, but in three months
he has lost two jobs when his lie was discovered. Nobody will
take a chance on him, Lord.

In prison he met a lot of people and only You know how it
scares me to think they will get together. All of them need
money and they're thrown upon a society reluctant to receive
them.

"I've paid my debt," he pleaded to his last boss. "Give me a
chance." But the boss was afraid for the reputation of his
shop.

One day on the street I met the lawyer who defended Jack
five-and-a-half years ago. At the time he was genuinely sorry
that the sentence was so tough. Remember, Lord, how I explained our current plight? He volunteered to ask around
about jobs but nothing came of it.

I asked our preacher if he knew anyone who would "take a
chance." He offered Jack a job as church custodian and yard

man. Thank You for making this opening, Jack took it but
hoped to return to barbering. Twice the preacher tried to
arrange opportunities for barbering but with excuses the
shops reneged their offers.

Lord, our most important break came one night when the
preacher and two other men came to our home. One man was
the druggist on Wolcott Street and the other we knew by reputation as an excellent carpenter. We were greatly surprised
that both had prison records. Remember how timidly they
asked if Jack would be interested in becoming a member of a
group they were organizing to assist ex-convicts in reestablish-
ing themselves as first-class citizens?

"We have twelve men in town who are trying to make it
back but they're having difficulty."

"Why are you doing this?" Jack asked.

"Because we've been through it. It's tough without support."

O God, somebody understood. Thank You.

The preacher said it had something to do with reconciliation—that whenever people need help and are being treated as
outsiders it's time for reconciliation. "Right now we can help
each other. In days ahead we can help others." The men
agreed.

Before leaving they talked of a low-cost loan to help Jack
buy into a barber shop. They talked of several possibilities
and next Tuesday Jack is to meet them at the bank. I don't
know what will happen next, Lord. Something tells me You
worked it out. I know only that society isn't pinching us anymore and Jack doesn't walk like an untouchable.

*Stop buggin' about my hair.   Man, you're
hooked on trivia.*

I ADMIT IT, LORD, I'M SQUARE AS AN ICE CUBE AND
my son is a hippie.   I admit that too.   His defense reflexes
work twenty-four hours a day.

Sometimes we know where he is and when we don't we're
not to ask.   I've almost given up praying about him, Lord.
Anything we believe, he automatically turns off.   "Family
traditions are old and dumb," he says.   "Get with it and do
your thing."

Lord, for twenty-six years I've thought "my thing" was
maintaining a home and raising three sons.   I have loved it.
We live in a nice town full of fine people.   You know.   Most
of us believe the American flag is a symbol of freedom our
forefathers fought for and I get tears in my eyes over "The
Star-Spangled Banner."   Most of us believe in the joys of
family living where love is sacred and through it children grow
into mature and morally responsible human beings.   Most of
us believe in hard work which reaps dividends of home ownership, a car, and ample security.   At journey's end we will leave
these material gifts gladly to our children.

Lord, are You listening when he talks?

"Patriotism," our son says, "is a middle class hang-up sold us
by crafty politicians.   The only thing truly American is rebellion.   Look at history and you'll see real revolutions—not
peaceful demonstrations."

"Sex," he says, "should be as free as breathing and nobody

45

should be a holdout for marriage. That's old and dumb too."

On material possessions he says, "They keep people grounded. Who needs 'em?"

On family, he maintains that everybody is his family. We answer, "That's not what you practice. You accept only those who think like you. The rest of us are segregated out."

On drugs he says, "Don't knock it 'til you've tried it."

We go round and round, Lord. His thought process is based in a port foreign to ours. As we see it, he has no ambition to be anybody, do anything, or contribute positively to the building of a better community—world community or otherwise.

We have spent hours guiltily scraping the past hoping to spot where we went wrong. Our emotions have bounced between hurt, anger, frustration, disappointment, and futility. Reading on the subject has been helpful at the point of understanding the problem but not solving it. We talked with his high-school guidance counselor and learned that many youth think this way. By contacting him we also learned, at least, we weren't alone. Other parents were floundering too.

We've almost had it, Lord. For months we've been dangling loose from the situation admitting he doesn't need us now and may never again need us. Pressing him on any subject simply agitates argument.

The situation is status quo. I shall go on being me and "doin' my thing." He will go on doing his. If we meet at the corner of need—wonderful. If not, then let it be.

Madame, don't panic. As you can see I'm black, am holding $2500 in cash for down payment, and the Civil Liberties Union is behind me. There is no alternative but to sell me your house in this white neighborhood.

HE WAS RIGHT. HE HAD THE MONEY, THE LAW, AND the backing but panic I did. Lord, do You remember how I panicked?

My home had been on the market for over a month. Prospects had come and gone without offers. For thirty years we had lived in this house and when Henry died I had no need of a five-bedroom two-story house with garage on one-and-a-half acres. In its time this had been the best white neighborhood in town.

I guess I am naïve, Lord. It never dawned on me that a blockbuster might want the house. Such things happen in other neighborhoods to other people.

"He's right," the realtor said. "Fair Housing laws support him all the way. Nothing you nor I can do will change that."

By morning the shock had worn off and all I could think was "What will the neighbors say?" I have never thought I was color prejudiced but the man's attitude upset me. His infuriating manner, Lord, brought out my disguised discrimination. I called my sons and at their suggestion I went to several close neighbors explaining what had happened. They were furious and talked petitions and court hearings.

None of us thought we were prejudiced against blacks. We

47

were prejudiced against the pressure of this particular black.

Neighbors suggested I call an attorney and I did.

"Fair Housing laws are unbendable," he said.

"But if he has freedom to buy wherever he wants, do I not have freedom to sell to whomever I want?"

"No," came the attorney's reply.

"What if I take my house off the market and decide not to sell?"

"It wouldn't stand up. There'd be too much evidence of bad faith when the house has been up for sale this long."

"Don't I have any rights?" I asked.

"Yes, one possible loophole. List carefully every defect in the house—loose bricks, cracked plaster, old plumbing, outdated wiring—anything that makes a buyer stop and think twice. Send the original copy of it to the realtor and a copy to me.

My sons came and we listed carefully every defect. The neighbors were tense. People I had known for thirty years were suddenly hostile, but I informed them of my one possible loophole.

Within two days the realtor appeared carrying the letter of listed defects. He checked each one and called that evening to say the prospect had backed out.

Lord, it was for me a cruel initiation into discrimination. On one side the tentacles of fair housing were squeezing the breath out of me and on the other there was massive watching by my neighbors. I still have the house, the realtor still has the list, and the neighborhood has raised an antenna for racial pressure. Above all, Lord, I am left with a guilty conscience over the whole proceeding.

Around midnight I smelled smoke. Easy inspection yielded nothing. The neighborhood was not in flames so I went back to bed. Before dawn our family was routed by screaming sirens to an unbelievable quirk of circumstances which left us homeless.

EMOTIONALLY LORD, WE PASSED THROUGH FRIGHT TO thankfulness for safety then to despair over our loss. The children finally stopped crying, but as weeks passed our outer emergencies gave way to inner ones.

Our material loss was total. Even the insurance company said so. In the confines of a motel we pieced the night together, giving thanks for an aroused neighbor who saw flames where three hours earlier I had smelled smoke.

Fire had consumed our past and present, Lord. Only You knew the future. In the attic we lost a little rocker belonging to my grandmother, a beautiful doll carefully wrapped to ward off dust, several boxes of old sheet music, and my husband's baby cradle. Irreplaceables. We lost family pictures of our toddlers, of picnics and vacations, to say nothing of all our clothing and furniture.

Now after a year I am rebuilding myself mentally and spiritually, Lord, realizing we lost only the portables and can backtrack to the point of replacing some of them. The other things were exactly that—t-h-i-n-g-s. If I hadn't had the rocker, You know, I would continued to cherish my grandmother anyway. My love for her had nothing to do with the rocker.

The rocker was esteemed because she had used it, and it seemed like a little piece of her still with me. But, Lord, You knew how much I loved her long before I inherited the rocker, and the chair still has nothing to do with my lively memory of her.

As for pictures of the children, we are gathering some here and there from relatives and friends who snapped a few.

Lord, my whole philosophy concerning material possessions has changed. True, I was forced into it but the change in attitude on "things" has been my greatest rescue squad. Things are symbolic ties to relationships. They keep us sensitive—sometimes too sensitive. They are gentle reminders as the years flake away. Without them my memory may work overtime to recapture moments but I haven't lost the essense of the wonderful past.

I have become less possessive. I buy less and sort more in order to avoid stockpiling. My new home is simple and functional. When I see stuffed closets and drawers, it's time to sort —not time to add a room.

Lord, You know I have become more acutely aware of human emergencies, and I jump in to help instead of waiting for an organization to make a public appeal. A blanket here or a few dishes there mean more than I ever realized.

Our fire was caused by bad wiring not by You trying to give me wisdom. But out of the experiences, Lord, our family has grown closer, more protective of each other, more disturbed over the emergencies of others, more sensible over material losses, and more thankful over spiritual gains.

I'm a conformist and know it. Too much individuality leads to criticism I don't want. Slowly, I'm realizing it's easier to be with the majority but harder to maintain a personal value system. What do I do now?

LORD, YOU KNOW I'M THE LAST TO JUMP ON A BAND-wagon, but I would rather get on than speak my mind for not getting on. Sometimes I'm herded into an attitude by people who talk louder and think faster.

"Get with it. Nobody buys alcoholic temperance anymore. It's a leftover from somebody's archaic notion about sin."

I winced.

A verbal answer invited criticism and I swerved, but lately I feel pressure pinched to accept the moral changing of the guard. My reason, Lord, for not drinking is simple. It was tattooed on my mind that drinking was a sin. Once my grand-mother needed ice cream and the only place open was a tavern. Being a teetotaler, she felt it was sinful to go inside. They sold her a quart of chocolate ice cream at the front door. That is my heritage on the subject of alcohol.

"Social acceptance doesn't make it right," I could have said.

"Chalk it up to the changing times," I should have said.

"Stop bugging me," I wanted to say.

My friends drink socially. I enjoy them in spite of it and don't want to be left out of their activities. I do not want to be the only party prude reaching for tomato juice. Lord, neither do I want to be kidded as the only holdout against "social" progress.

My husband joined the rising cocktail cult on the rumor that it helped business. He said he felt like Jonah being swallowed by the whale.

Corny as it sounds, Lord, I have to be me. I believe there is still such a thing as being true to my best self. Along with the crowd I can change my hems, zigzag my politics, buy a wig, or take up skindiving, but if the latest social customs make me sell my best self short, I've been oversold on conformity.

At present, Lord, I'm stabilizing myself on the thought that real friendship isn't tucked in by whether people drink, but underneath I know the social games people play do have a way of polarizing friendship.

Mother, stop being naïvely patriotic. American justice needs a fat overhaul, and until somebody mocks it out publicly, injustice keeps jailing the poor and bailing the rich.

LORD, YOU KNOW HOW HARD I TRIED NOT TO BE IRKED over her label on my bankrupt vision of patriotism. Youth's greatest flaw is its total ineptitude in dealing with parents. The generation gap could be all washed up with a little bedrock diplomacy, but everybody comes on throwing stones.

On people over twenty, "You're using old agendas for the new order," my daughter says.

On elections, "Time to play political musical chairs."

On Congress she says, "Useless as a burnt match."

Lord, to her the legal system is put together by egg beaters. The inequities in sentencing, drafting, bailing, and among judges themselves give her a case of political indigestion and she says it loud and clear.

Shinanigans at the trial of the Chicago Seven kept her glued to newscasts for weeks while her weekends were spent boycotting grapes in supermarkets.

She calls herself an American patriot. Her old clothes symbolize hard work and rejection of affluent America. She hasn't bought a dress for two years, but recently at our insistence she wore one to a neighbor's funeral.

Hoping better to understand her ideas, Lord, I read the brochures she leaves around and discuss them with her at times other than dinner.

53

Her father flies into a tizzy at her far-out philosophy, says she doesn't know what she's talking about, and waves the red, white, and blue at her. Either she turns him off or tries to outshout him.

Lord, in dealing with this I've asked her to bring home her friends, and once I timidly opened our rec room for their activities. Afterward I spent two days getting poster paint off the floor, sweeping out ashes, and generally fumigating.

"You're oversold on conformity," she said.

I tried to point out that she dressed, thought, acted, and looked like her "in" crowd but was told that it isn't conformity, it's unity.

Not all youth think like our daughter. Suggested solutions of friends have run from "Send her to a convent" to "Cut her financial leash." Lord, I'm stumped and admit it.

After reading her literature, discussing things with her when I'm allowed, offering her gang the rec room, consulting with other parents, and eavesdropping on youth today, I realize I'm only treading water and getting nowhere. Lord, what do I do now?

My convictions and age won't let me join them, so I'll sit this out, keep on loving her, and hope she won't drop us because we're over twenty.

What is sin anyway? I used to think it was card playing, drinking, and dancing. Today it's a whole new bag—like allowing slums and starvation to exist in my community.

LORD, TO ME, ONE OF THE GREATEST SINS IS TO BE aware that something is evil and then consciously close our eyes, pretend it isn't there, and hope it will go away.

Once I thought sin changed with parental whim.

Then I thought it changed with the times.

Now, Lord, I think sin is facing evil and doing nothing— like allowing social conditions to exist which keep people from living as human beings. War, poverty, starvation all fall into this category and the breadth of these has matured by religious thinking.

Don't get me wrong, Lord. I'm no crusader. Most of us have a knack for adjusting blinders when we see social problems.

I don't want to get involved.

Keep me posted on what you're doing. Maybe I'll come around.

Can't help. That's not my dish.

Let welfare do it.

I couldn't care less.

People aren't being flip with these comments, Lord. They are being truthful and cruel.

The New Testament demands that I act on my new consciousness—to reach people in need and lift them to a place where they may productively contribute to society. This takes imagination, resources, and dedication but I can't ignite much of it in others.

At first I thought everybody, by nature, had social awareness. I was wrong, Lord. That idea gave way to the thought that everybody *could* have it if they were educated on deplorable conditions but education by brochure is a slow nitty-gritty so I gave up in favor of involvement. I worked on the theory, Lord, that involvement leads to understanding and understanding leads to solutions.

My telephone became a veritable hot line urgently trying to recruit volunteers for involvement, but getting volunteers is as hard as spooning out the Pacific.

"It's sinful to allow people to live like that in our town," I would say and with great sincerity the answer would rise and die, "Yes, it is." Thus endeth the conversation.

In the process, Lord, I realized I had more zeal than know-how. So I have pulled in my lust for morality and volunteered myself for a tutoring program where adults from hard-core poverty are learning to read and write. It's exciting to see them become literate citizens.

Last week the president of our Women's Guild at the church called to ask if I would tell about the tutoring program. Who knows, maybe You will work through me to get a few more volunteers for tutoring.

My son is a high-school dropout. He is lazy, jobless, and presently in jail for forgery. Three times in two months we were summoned by police in the middle of the night. Twice we bailed him out and made good on the checks. The third time we didn't.

A TELLER DISCOVERED HIS FORGERY, LORD, AND PRESSED an undercounter button to summon a guard.

Passing bad checks supplemented what Eddie's laboring job didn't pay. For several years we had warned, threatened, and shamed but his habits didn't change. Nothing phased him.

"So what?" he would say.

"If you don't care for yourself think of us. We have a business in this town and a reputation to uphold."

"So?"

"So your behavior is important to us. The first time the judge warned, next you got off lucky with a suspended sentence. Next you'll do time."

"Not long."

"Long enough I hope to knock some sense into your head," his father said.

"Nobody makes it without money."

"Nobody makes it without being trustworthy. You'll regret a jail record as long as you live."

"So who's livin'?"

"You could be. You've had a fine home, several good jobs, and all the opportunity in the world to amount to something. You're blowing it."

Around they went, Lord—neither sidestepping nor gaining.

Ed was furious when we refused to post bail. His fury was the only sign of determination we had seen in him for some time. We were as determined.

His checks had been small enough to slide by unsuspecting tellers but large enough to be lucrative. Small successes generated larger checks and more frequent attempts.

Worried, we consulted an attorney who agreed to defend Ed. He was doubtful that he could get Ed off lightly and said if the sentence was stiff we should appeal.

"No appeal," my husband said without faltering.

"No appeal," I voiced limply.

We accompanied the attorney to the county jail where he told Ed his sentence could be as much as four years. Lord, it was then we told him we loved him, would do anything short of getting him off with parental pleas, and would not allow his sentence to be appealed. You know, Lord, our decision had come through hours of sleeplessness, discussion, prayer, and thought.

"My old man is gonna teach me a lesson," Ed said to the attorney.

"No, Ed, that's the trouble. We've never been able to teach you anything."

"We'll stick by you son," I said.

"Stick by with a file in a cake, will ya mom?"

He drew four years without early probation. We go on visiting days. He looks like a tame rabbit and talks about the future. Some of the men he associates with are hard-core criminals, and often we whip ourselves over the coldheartedness of our decision not to appeal.

The years are passing, Lord, and in about fifteen more we plan to retire. As perpetually hopeful parents we expect to turn our business over to a son whose greatest occupational hazard may be a jail record.

Already I have a chain across the door, sir.
Now I need a lock that slides across the door
jamb and locks with a key.
The clerk knew what I wanted.

I'M AFRAID AT NIGHT. YOU KNOW I ADMIT IT, LORD. My husband travels for his company and being alone makes me jittery.

The neighborhood has organized against crime, which is some mental security, but I'm still afraid. No one walks his dog after dark. Every block has a blue star window sign designating a mother who will be home after school in case a child needs help. Oldsters have changed their club meetings from night to afternoon. We notify neighbors when we're going away and check that the paperboy, mailman, and milkman have been notified. Most of us have timers on lights. Everyone has been encouraged to get to know at least one neighbor and tape her number to the telephone.

Lord, fear isn't new to me. It has been hiding in me from childhood, but rising crime rates on thieves and muggers don't help. I have never been robbed. No one I know has ever been robbed or mugged. It is fear of what *might* happen that creates anxiety.

You know, Lord, that within the past six months I have initiated a self-strengthening program instigated by a TV panel on "Getting More Out of Life." My adaptation of their idea is something like this:

1. Stop picturing myself as a victim of crime. Stop imagining the worst and stop imagining that every crime is happening to me.

2. Excitement over reported crimes may be natural nervousness but not fear. There is a difference and I need to sort it out.

3. Try to be more self-reliant, keep active, and keep myself thinking positively not negatively.

4. I, alone, have power over this.

Changing the image of myself, Lord, is chiseling away at my weaknesses in order to rearrange the foundation stones of my strengths. I feel more relaxed at night. The growing uneasiness is gone. In the morning I feel more alert, more active and stimulated to work in the yard or meet friends for fun. I make myself leave the house for awhile each day.

These ideas are working for me, Lord. They do make a difference.

The time will never come when I would rather be alone than have my husband home, but he would be furious if he thought coming home was only to protect me from the bogeyman.

I used to believe a lot of things I'm now doubting. I feel guilty and am afraid I'm losing my religious faith.

REMEMBER THE CONVERSATION, LORD?

"You're spring cleaning," my husband said. "There's nothing wrong with sorting your mental closet."

"Maybe I'm throwing out things I'll need."

"Yep, it's possible but I doubt it. We save more than we ever need. It's the squirrel in us."

"The funny thing is I don't even want to do it. It's happening in spite of me."

"Then don't let it happen. Don't listen to the news, don't read anything, don't talk with anybody, don't think. Are you saying you have everything in little mental boxes and you don't want them opened, touched, or shaken?"

"Yes."

"Then how do you expect to use the contents?"

"Everything is there if I need it."

"But we need it every day. We need every solid handle we can grab just to keep in the safety zone. Life today is like waltzing with a time bomb, and if you've stashed away anything usable against daily fallout, sit up all night and guard it if you have to. But keep it in working order," he said.

"You're getting awfully excited over my little mental spring cleaning."

"Because suddenly I see how calm you are about it and it scares me. This isn't an age to take a couple of aspirins, hoping our headaches will go away. If your little boxes need sorting, get to it and don't be afraid or guilty. Our security has to be solid rock not little pebbles rattling in boxes."

"I never saw you so serious."

"I never saw you dillydally over important matters. Listen, if prayer is part of your security take it out and look at it under a microscope. Do you really believe Someone listens when you pray? What kind of Someone? What do you really believe about Him? Is He always good or does He sometimes create evil? Is everything that happens in the world His will? Then why do people get sick and suffer? Work these out in your mind. Get them in place so all of it makes sense to you. That's all I'm saying."

"Of course I believe in God. But some of those questions I've hated to ask out loud."

"Why?"

"Because it seems like I'm doubting religion and that isn't right."

"Doubts are healthy. If St. Paul hadn't doubted he would have stayed a Jew. If St. Augustine hadn't doubted he would have been an agnostic the rest of his life. If St. Francis hadn't doubted he would have spent his life as a rich patrician. Just today, if I hadn't doubted my figures until proven right, a bridge might have fallen. If doctors didn't doubt that a disease was incurable, they would give up. If scientists hadn't doubted that man was glued to the earth, we wouldn't have made it to the moon. Doubts are a generator for thought and action. Without them we would have to be pulled on strings like puppets, and my guess is that was far from God's intention when he created man."

"Okay, I get your point."

I'm exhausted from arguing with him. Between my short fuse and his spending like there's no tomorrow marriage is an everlasting skirmish.

LORD, HIS IDEA OF MONEY IS AN ECONOMIC DISASTER area, and every time I think about the guy who invented credit cards, it raises my metabolism.

My husband buys anything (which he doesn't need), charges it (which we can't afford), and changes jobs (which promise to make him more with less work). In the past two years he has sold cars, worked construction, and driven a semi in interstate trucking. He says he is doing it for the family and does bring home more money. Along with it he brings home more debts and more overdrafts at the bank.

You know, Lord, I have talked, pleaded, and argued with him and compromised to handle our finances if he promises to tear up his credit cards. He hits the ceiling saying, "No woman is going to handle my money!"

Once I approached his boss hoping to intercept his paycheck and pay our bills, but it didn't work. The boss saw Ed as a happy-go-lucky big spender entertaining the boys and saw me as a meddling old biddy.

Buying seems compulsive with him, Lord. I tell him it's because he never had anything and every time he gets anything he tries to play the big shot. "I earn it so hang loose, woman!" That's his answer.

He has to be seen and is loud on the street, at work, and at home until somebody yells, "Knock it off."

In early years he dreamed big on his instant personality. People hired him on his appeal and good looks. In those years, Lord, I really believe he was doing it for the family. Now he seems to be doing it because he can't help it. He pushes harder and louder to make a bigger splash.

At first, I thought of getting police pressure to make him pay our bills. Then I considered an attorney but gave it up fearing a lot of legal things would get me a divorce I didn't want.

Lord, You know how carefully I listed people who could help objectively, listen closely, advise patiently, and not gossip the problem all over town. I sought out a Catholic priest I'd never seen in a church I'd never attended. After pondering three days I went.

He was wonderful, Lord. We talked alternatives of action; even visited the bank to investigate whether I could stop action on our joint account each month until debts are paid.

His most important help came at a point completely foreign to me—that Ed might need a psychiatrist. Laughingly, I agreed. "Don't we all!" But he meant what he said and pointed out angles of Ed's personality which sounded askew.

"How can I pay for one? They charge an arm and a leg."

"There's a Mental Health Center here. The professional staff comes fifty miles each Friday from a big hospital. There is a waiting list but referrals are made by police, clergy, doctors, and the judge. Maybe your best bet is allowing Ed to run a few more debts and the judge will refer him quickly enough if you explain his wider pattern of behavior. The Center is maintained by the United Fund and charges people only if they can pay."

Lord, the whole idea was new, but it was a good one. At present it is bringing me peace of mind. Soon it may guarantee my future, too.

We have one car and four drivers. Three are teen-agers. For awhile I was deluged with offers to pick up the dry cleaning, return a book, or take the cat to the vet. Now the family is in a constant tizzy over whose turn it is to use the car.

LORD, IT WOULD SEEM THAT FIVE INTELLIGENT PEOPLE should be able to solve this with more output from the family power plant, but at this point it would be easier to pull the plug on the gas tank or park the car in cold storage.

The kids have tried every trick. They hide the keys from each other, make up emergencies which prevent them from getting the car home, call in excuses, trade times without consulting the other guy, and gripe over paying for gas that somebody else uses.

We have teased, threatened, and bribed but nothing seems to help. A long burst of temper on the subject isn't any more effective than a short one.

Our only asset, Lord, is having nearly free repairs because the boys do it themselves. Hope runs high that in another year two boys can muster enough money to buy a car and enough brotherly love to share it.

Recently the boys wrote the following commandments for car use:

1. Thou shalt not expect Dad to pay for gas.

2. Thou shalt not paint it purple, striped or decorate in any other way without family vote.

65

3. Thou shalt not use the trunk as a floating closet.

4. Thou shalt not loan the car to girls or other irresponsible creatures.

5. Thou shalt get the car home on time without spinning false tales of woe.

Scared is an understatement. I'm petrified.
The children are not safe as long as he stays
around here.

ALCOHOL IS MY FATHER'S PROBLEM, LORD, BUT IT practically spills over our entire family. He is a Dr. Jekyll or Mr. Hyde depending on his state of drunkenness. Long ago Mother gave up trying to diagnose why he drank and arrived at the crossroads of what to do with him and how to protect us kids from him.

Lord, running away with us looked easy but financially and legally running away is her most difficult route. She has been to the preacher, police, and doctor (all helpful at various times). Members of Alcoholics Anonymous have been wonderful. She sloughs off neighborly and family pity because the situation is beyond it. She has heard him labeled no good, bum, and fink plus a lot of unrepeatables.

She labels him as sick and for years her label meant physical illness. Twice he has taken the "cure" but it didn't work.

Recently, Lord, she watched a TV special on the alcoholic. Most of the show was aimed at mental illness. The approach was a new avenue for her and for him.

Now decision is at hand. Lord, it takes her signature and two doctors' to commit him to a mental hospital.

She is afraid of him and hates the possibility of kids teasing us with "Your-daddy-is-you-know-where." My dad's parents are fighting it, too. She knows, Lord, that for him it might mean health, but it might be that he would hate her for taking such a step. In time it would mean hearing his promises of reform all over again with pleas for another chance. She isn't sure she wants another chance with him.

Help her decide, Lord. Night and day she keeps asking, "What do I do now?"

*Your baby is a mongoloid. How badly I do
not know. Only time and tests will show.*

THE SHOCK WAS THERE, LORD, BUT BEING YOUNG AND
full of hope we expected to conquer the situation with love
and medical miracles.

Immediately the doctor pointed out to us his enlarged head
and wide-set eyes. The doctor then picked up Billy with one
hand. The baby lay limp with drooping head and legs instead of kicking and fighting to raise himself. We saw and
accepted.

The doctor talked of tests, drugs, and observation periods
offered by centers specializing in retardation. We asked questions for which there were no answers. We got answers for
questions we had not known to ask.

Time passed, Lord, and at four years Billy was not unlike a
newborn. His measureable IQ was very low and we gave up
hope that he could participate in society. Once the doctor
suggested residential care which, to me, was out of the question. "Never!" I exclaimed. "No institutions for my son.
Billy was given to us and needs us. We will fulfill our responsibility."

At ten, Lord, he could walk but could not care for himself
physically. With great trouble he fed himself. Inside the
house, I watched every minute for fear he would hurt himself. Outside, I watched for fear other children would hurt
him. He cried easily and with whimpers extended his arms
for everything he couldn't manage. He was totally dependent

69

on me, Lord, and only You would understand what that means. Discipline should have been given but I substituted pity.

During the summers we sent him to day camp where one counselor was assigned to him. Lord, wasn't she wonderful? She didn't even mind his wet kisses. Intuitively, she grew to anticipate his needs before frustration set in.

At twenty he was still full-time care. Physically he was strong and healthy. Mentally he was about eight, which was to be his maximum.

Now, Lord, we are in the grip of making legal provisions on the occasion of our deaths. We are caught on the horns of a two-pronged dilemma.

We have agreed that Billy will require institutional care. If we place him soon, it will be hard for us but we could help him adjust. Waiting until our deaths would be easier for us but harder on him.

We are weighing, also, the advantages and disadvantages of public versus private care. Public is cheaper but it is run like a jail. Private is expensive but we could visit at will and take him for long weekends. The public institution exists on taxes and won't go out of business. The private exists on small endowments and grants. What happens to patients if money runs out and the place is forced to close?

O Lord, hardest of all is knowing that Billy won't be in our home. Every day for twenty-three years I have had him here. Not having him throws me against the realities of grief and into the necessity of starting life again. O God, help me. I am convinced I cannot cope with this.

GALA NITE
Dinner-Dance

Hawaiian Room   Plaza Hotel

"COUPLES ONLY"

ANOTHER INVITATION FOR COUPLES ONLY! A SINGLE woman at fifty years, I was trapped like a fly at the window who sees out but can't find the way. Lord, the world seemed to be set up for couples. I told myself that ever since Noah everything goes two by two. It was infuriating to me.

For couples, invitations from the club were for night beach parties, barbecues, and overnights at the lodge. For single people, invitations from the club offered field trips through the stock yards or slides on early printing presses or book reviews on basket weaving.

It wasn't that marriage looked perfect, Lord. At work I saw plenty of hanky-panky at the water cooler, and privately I sorted out the marrieds who had a carnival on business trips.

71

Over the years my emotions on being single ran from little disappointments to a big case of self-pity. First there was disappointment. (Wish I could go to the dance.) Disappointment moved toward being frantic. (But I don't want to live alone forever.) Frantic moved into sour grapes. (I'd rather be free anyway.) Sour grapes turned into self-pity. (There's nothing special about me so I can't be special to anyone.) Self-pity went to complacency. (Oh well—maybe it was meant to be.)

Lord, not until forty did it dawn on me that single people are unique. They haven't been shortchanged. To think they have is a social hand-me-down idea. Neither are they grounded. They have social freedom to soar. When I felt jailed I did it to myself.

Four years ago with this philosophy I bought a modest little home. Friends thought it commendable but impractical. I sold a lot of my old furniture, painted some, and bought a little. Life started over at forty-six. I bought a car and during my first vacation drove no farther than the other side of the county to see people I hadn't seen in years.

My new neighborhood gave me a broader outlook. It was different from the apartment-living concept of neighborliness. Many of my favorite back-door visitors were less than eight years old.

For years, Lord, I had been building a social-psychic roadblock on being single. Instead of analyzing the situation and breaking through, I was in my frenzy digging a rut beside the roadblock.

Today I accept the fact that I am single and do not make apologies for it because for me, Lord, being single has blessings all its own.

*She has suffered terribly and soon there will
be three children to care for.*

TWENTY-TWO MONTHS AGO, WITH GREAT COMPOSURE
my sister told us she had cancer. Lord, we were heartbroken
for her, for her husband, and for her children. Her health
had been unusually good. While she was on vacation she
noticed a sudden growth. Extensive treatments followed an
operation but the malignancy could not be contained.

How could we face this? How could we tell the children?
O God, do you recall our panic?

Alone, she has worked it out for us. Throughout the experience she has been a deep and abiding blessing to all of
us. Her faith in You and the wholeness of life has helped us
accept and adapt to the forthcoming changes.

"Isn't there another serum, another treatment?" I asked.
"Is everything gone but hope?"

"Hope is at the beginning and the end, Carrie," she said.
"He must have planned it that way. Hope is the very fiber
pulling man's pains and pleasures into a carefully synchronized
pattern. You think of it merely as the last trump by which
we win or lose, but with hope man has done everything from
catch his first glimpse of a star through a telescope to counting
specks of pollen on a bee. For me hope is the beginning, not
the end."

"But this isn't the beginning. It is the end," I said tearfully.

"The end of what, Carrie—the end of my little earth

73

journey? Is it really so significant that I finish before you and Ed? Nothing is ever completely finished, you know. God isn't wasteful. When a leaf falls it's only preparing to change shape.

"Hope does more than spring eternal in the human breast, Carrie. It is the very essense of life itself and man succeeds or fails during his days on the strength of its pulse. Don't lose hope, Carrie, because then you've lost me.

"Fighting for life is more than fighting with pills and treatments. It's fighting with fresh hope each morning that when death comes it's only the eternity in life changing shape."

Lord, on the strength of such faith she has taught us to face the fact of her coming death. During such conversations with our family and close friends she is carving a delicate and incredible heritage while walking through the valley of the shadow.

The roads are now unsafe at any speed. Tomorrow my son will leap behind the wheel and rise to his utopia as a licensed driver.

THE CAR HAS BEEN TESTED, LORD, FOR GOOD BRAKES, balanced tires, strong horn, bright lights, accurate speed, ample battery, and sturdy shock absorbers. My son has been tested on how well he memorized the driving manual last night.

We get no money-back guarantee if he doesn't have an accident; we twinge over sky-rocketing insurance rates; we gripe over being grounded. We will gasp everytime the phone rings for fear he is a statistic, and from here on we will be pelted with excuses to get the car.

We have the feeling that tomorrow introduces us into a new subculture where archaic notions about needing parents are traded for superrigged chrome and long-range promises to be home for supper.

Lord, remember about a year ago how greatly concerned we were over Bill's lack of a sense of responsibility for safe driving? After a lot of talk and red-hot arguments we made a deal with him. If for one year he could maintain a driving record without bumps, bruises, dents, fines, warnings, or lawsuits, we would get him a car of his own. He was jubilant and kept saying, "Cool, man. That's real cool."

His record had been spotless and once he even volunteered to wash the car. Now I ride with my eyes open and fists unclenched. He is a good boy, Lord, and a responsible driver.

Oddly enough, for the past month he has used the car very little. Sometimes he walks. Sometimes he is picked up by friends in jalopies or on motor bikes. We have thought it strange.

Last night, Lord, solemn as a judge, he said his year of safety was over and instead of a car could he have a motor bike?

Congratulations, you're pregnant. Pregnant! But doctor. I'm forty-five with two teen-agers.

HE DIDN'T PUSSYFOOT AND I WAS DISSOLVED IN TEARS. Lord, the last thing I wanted was to start over.

Shock waves rolled into waves of embarrassment guessing what people would say. Having an unplanned baby at forty-five didn't seem quite the thrill of having one at twenty. I hated giving up my friends to be leashed to a tight baby schedule, and the thought of night feedings, excessive laundry, sitters, and formulas left me numb. Who needed it at my age?

I decided not to tell—maybe for three or four months. After all, nobody had to know and I could try to ignore it awhile. This lasted three days, Lord. I told the family and a few close friends. The news spread like the measles. Every private secret weapon I had was shot down. My husband was so happily spreading the news I lightheartedly threatened to burn the marriage license and refuse to participate.

Underneath his joy was my less than joyful mind-set. Slyly, I blamed him for recklessness and me for apathy. In fact I told him he was excited because it proved his youthfulness. Also, I may have felt guilty because most middle-aged couples don't get caught. We were certainly old enough to avoid this crisis and to me it was just that.

The children were floored, then slowly receptive. They were not jubilant as smaller children would have been.

Lord, in self-study realization came that it was not having

77

the baby but raising it that got me uptight. With the other two each stage had been an exciting surprise. Thoughts of another playpen in the living room, a swing set in the yard, and another round at PTA was too much. With such thoughts I worked myself into a noticeable first-class depression. My doctor had a fit. So did my husband but both were surprisingly sympathetic.

I balked for nine long months. Now after a year I thrive on such comments as, "You're so relaxed and efficient with him." "You look ten years younger." "The Lord sure knew who to send him to." Come to think of it, Lord, it's people-to-me resusitation that is pulling me through.

What's all this about Bishop Pike speaking with his dead son? And Bishop Pike being met by Dr. Tillich after death? Come on now . . .

FORGIVE ME, LORD, IF I SEEM SHORTSIGHTED. I'M AS game as the next to take up new ideas but in this I'm ungullable. The whole thing turns me off.

"Don't talk yourself into a corner on it," my friend said. "We're on the moon, aren't we?"

"What does the moon have to do with it?"

"It's a miracle, too."

"The moon landing isn't a miracle. It's science."

"You stick to yours and I'll stick to mine."

"Your what?"

"My idea that a lot of science is a miracle and a lot of miracle is probably science if we were only smart enough to decipher it. There are reasons for things happening even things like receiving messages through mediums or ESP."

"Do you believe in ESP?" I asked.

"I believe in God."

"What does God have to do with ESP?"

"I believe in a Creator-God who has filled the universe with so many mysteries that most of them we haven't yet wondered about. To me they are miracles. Some of them man may never work out even if he spends forever and ever in his scientific labs. Maybe some he will—things like ESP, communication with the dead, intuition, and animal language.

We know these things do exist and people do experience them, but they belong to a realm of science we know little about. Nowadays when mysterious things happen we can laugh them off or accept them as realities we can't explain. To me they are miracles."

"To me they are tricks of the mind—wish fulfillments and all that," I said.

"To each her own. Maybe memory is a trick of the mind, too, but we've learned a lot about it and science even improved on it by storing information in a computer."

Lord, that conversation took place six months ago and I have been stirred up ever since. My conclusion is that what I want to believe with my heart I can't always accept with my mind, and by the time I accept it with my mind the mystery is all gone. Maybe You meant for us to keep a delicate balance between wonder and logic.

I thought worship was supposed to be quiet and meditative, with soft organ music and hymns. Suddenly I've wound up with a generation gaposis and a dead inner battery.

AT FIRST IT WAS FUN. I ENJOYED THE FOLK MUSIC and young guitarists. Singing church-sounding words to "Michael Row the Boat Ashore" wasn't bad either.

On Sunday morning we had contemporary drama. It was an enjoyable experience but to me, Lord, not a worship experience.

Another Sunday we saw a film and divided into discussion groups. Talk was casual and stimulating. It led me to think but not to worship.

At first, Lord, I thought the changes were an attendance gimmick, but attendance stayed about the same. Then I thought it was to make our youth feel more at home, but few came unless they were participating. Now I have a hunch it's a passing fad, but underneath I'm afraid it's not.

"For you, what does morning worship have to have?" my preacher asked.

"I need quiet, thoughtful prayer, familiar hymns, the choir, and your sermon."

"That is the established pattern for many of us, but of course it doesn't mean that it is the only pattern," he said.

"I know. I'm trying to be open-minded. It isn't that people can't worship with new patterns. It's that I'm in a new

81

port. The surroundings are foreign to me and totally un-related to my life-long worship experience."

"That's true of everybody over eighteen. As a preacher it's not my intention to force one worship mold on everybody, but it seems like our era is a kaleidoscope and one mold doesn't fit anymore. There are days when I talk with people who are convinced that salvation comes by legislation. Some think sin is a church-patented booby trap. Others expect brotherhood by ladling out welfare and some see the church as an irrelevant security blanket. Today it takes every waking moment to keep updating ourselves and the church."

"If I didn't know you so well I'd think you are calling me old-fashioned."

"Today anybody over twenty is old-fashioned and we have to help people see that worship can be sedate to elaborately ceremonial or casual to leisurely, but whatever it is, people are meant to fall in love with each other and with God. Worship can't be dreary and monotonous. It has to be a stimulating experience of the spirit."

"Maybe we'll wind up having worship experiences like the different programs we offer different age groups the rest of the week. Maybe the youth could have their "thing" at 9:30 and the rest of us at 11:00."

"Or vice versa. On Sunday kids like to sleep late after Saturday night dates."

"You mean turn the eleven o'clock worship hour over to the youth?"

"What's so holy about 11 A.M.? We don't worship by punching a time clock."

We both laughed.

Lord, keep me steady in the winds of change but not rigid and unbending.

It's no good. We've been on the rocks for years. Let me go. You know I don't love you. We're done. Washed up.

WITH THREE TEEN-AGERS AND A MORTGAGE, LORD, IT was hard to see his reasoning. He was untrue. I knew it. Whether the kids guessed I didn't know. He paid the bills, came home at night when he wasn't on a "business trip," and generally played his role as man-of-the-house.

With timidity I visited a marriage consultant in a nearby city, so locally no one would know. We talked for an hour and he requested to see husband and wife together on the second visit. My husband wouldn't go, saying he didn't want to save the marriage and that counselors are always for saving the marriage.

Once I broke down and spilled the problem into the ear of a friend, but she was so prejudiced in my favor she lost objectivity and talking with her wasn't helpful.

Our minister felt marriage should be saved for the sake of the children and promised to see my husband. He did but was told by my husband to stop meddling. I was embarrassed about that, Lord.

My parents were crushed. His parents were furious with him. Neither were in positions to help me financially if I severed ties. Alimony wouldn't cover colleges, mortgage, insurance, and the cost of living.

I hired an attorney and the whole thing suddenly got as

complicated as D-Day. He explained and I accepted. He persuaded and I signed. Maybe I shouldn't have.

Lord, I never thought much about divorce. It's something that happens to movie stars and jet-setters—people totally unrelated to me. But here I am—confused, hurt, disappointed, tired, and lonely.

How are you? I asked. She told me and that was the beginning.

LORD, I HARDLY KNEW HER. SHE WAS ONE OF THE sparrow people (there are so many and they all look alike) whom I saw but didn't see. In my mind she didn't have a name, a street, a house, or a background. She was an older woman who slipped in and out of the same pew every Sunday almost unnoticed.

When I met her that day on the street, we talked. She was frail, Lord, very much alone and obviously not well.

Little by little I got involved with groceries, small errands, and now and then an invitation to Sunday dinner. As months went by she became increasingly dependent and I wanted to run.

I went to see the preacher. He knew my friend but not well. She was regular in church attendance but not active in the church program. We made guesses on her financial status. After some discussion we agreed to see her together. She was pleased to have us and a little relieved to think someone had her interest at heart. With gentle concern the preacher told her we wanted to help, but if we were to do so it meant facing a few facts. She agreed.

Financially, a nursing home was out of the question and retirement homes have waiting lists. Telephone calls proved it. The situation was not an emergency although within a year or so it would be. It would have been easier if it had been an emergency because a local hospital would have complied.

Lord, that which seemed a stalemate worked out for good.

The minister called together a group of seven women and two men from the congregation. He asked for help without time limit on the basis of love. The group worked quietly without organization, title, or recognition. For fourteen months they took turns providing one hot meal a day, repaired several nonfunctioning household items, and did errands. Several concerned neighbors pitched in. It was done without fanfare. At the end of fourteen months a church home accepted our friend.

Growing old had not made her bitter or complaining, Lord. It had simply made her very dependent. Her dependency was a crisis on our doorstep and when her need met our concern we rallied to help in Your name.

It's okay, don't worry. You son is a great guy and he can't get me pregnant because I take the pill.

THEY ARE SIXTEEN, LORD, AND HAVE GONE STEADY three months. Due to overcrowded conditions the high school is on split sessions and students are free by 12:30 each day. Some have jobs but part-time jobs are scarce.

I work everyday from eight to five to support my son and myself.

At dinner he was open about the fact that Alice had spent many afternoons at our home. They listened to records, ate, and often were joined by friends.

I became suspicious about sex when his bed was neatly made instead of thrown together as usual.

Timidity kept me from asking outright and I waited for a loophole that didn't come. Finally, I asked and he passed it off saying not to worry. He knew better than to get in trouble. I trusted him, Lord.

A week later I found myself alone with Alice while the boys changed tires on an old car. Mustering courage and blushing I slid into the subject of afternoon activities. She was way ahead of me and quickly said, "It's okay, don't worry. I take the pill."

Lord, I feel a moral obligation here. By my standard the situation calls for action, but any attempt to break up the relationship might drive it together.

I have thought about telling the girl's parents, but it might have the same effect because they might try to break it up. Talking it over with my son and his girl is not the answer either. It may cause them to run, saying that in the new morality love and sex are two entirely different things.

Lord, what do I do now?

I have lived on a farm all my life. I can forecast weather by signs in the sunset and flutter of leaves on trees. I can tell birds apart by their songs and know wild flowers by common name. But my life is changing. Little by little neighbors are selling off land to industry and like a giant leviathan the city is creeping in on me.

"IT'S COMING, MOM. WE MIGHT AS WELL FACE IT."
I think rural. My image of myself, Lord, is of a country woman who knows as much about the price of corn and how to bail hay as about canning eight bushels of tomatoes and raising pullets.

When I was little the neighbors helped each other shuck corn and thresh wheat. Now harvesting's done by equipment that cuts three thousand bushels of wheat in one half hour, and hay is cut, bailed, and stacked by one swoop of a mechanical goliath.

I remember when the mailman was traffic. Then two years ago the county blacktopped our road and delivery trucks erased the sounds of birds and took away my privacy.

My second son moved to town and the other son lives on a farm adjoining ours. He farms a little and works full time in a canning factory. My little granddaughters used to ride to my house on their pony. Now the road is too dangerous.

Last week we heard a rumor that an interstate highway is slated for a mile from here, which means moving the cemetery, and worst of all highways have a way of bringing motels and a hoard of littering tourists.

Lord, it wasn't hard to see the windmill go because we could pump water by electricity. It was even better when we sold the separator, started milking by electricity, and arranged for dairy truck pickup. It is true that with progress I finish my work faster, slip in a winter vacation, and watch TV. Industry has given me spare time I never dreamed of, but it is taking away my identity. Rural, as I have known it, is gone.

The stillness is gone, Lord. I can't hear the sound of corn whispering or the echo of a train whipping across the plains. Natural beauty is going, too, as the fields are slashed for highways and wired for progress. Clear morning air is disappearing with industry belching waste across the valley.

Lord, I have two choices. I can dry up in wistfulness hoping to turn back the hands of time or I can take a deep breath, store my rural image in a corner of wonderful memory, and start building a new identity.

My husband is antisocial. I hate to go out with him socially. He says he can't think of anything to say, can't relax, feels inferior. It makes me feel uneasy and him guilty.

"ANOTHER EVENING SHOT," HE SAID. "THEY DISCUSSED big business for two hours, argued politics for another, laughed over water cooler jokes, and polished off the evening by weight lifting. I can't do any of it and kept thinking of the time being wasted. I'm mad at myself and feel I'm cheating you."

Lord, I am a social butterfly and know it. He knew it, too, before we were married. I like people and am fed by them. They keep me revived for life. Social chitchat rolls out of me easily, and if a topic bounces beyond my intellectual recovery, I pitch questions.

"Don't be so sensitive. You're as smart as any man and you carry a responsible job dealing with people."

"That's different. Bookkeeping is exacting not creative. I can't create fun. I can't let go."

It was true that his feeling of inferiority buried his social creativity although at home he worked at creative hobbies finishing furniture and wood carving. "Both are hobbies of a loner," he never failed to point out.

Several days before a party he would get grumpy and turn on the silent treatment. By the time the event arrived, he attended physically but not mentally. He spent all evening wishing he were home and vowing secretly never to get caught at another party.

"You're uptight, Dad. Relax," the kids used to say.

At first, Lord, I swore off accepting social invitations. I didn't want to put him through a torture test to prove he loved me.

Then I accepted daytime events for women only. This was dull.

Once, by doing a good deed, I fell into a lucky idea. A friend was away so I invited her husband to join our family for dinner. He accepted. The men got along beautifully and wound up in the basement guessing the age of an antique pie safe which my husband was refinishing. Our guest had never heard of a pie safe, which gave my husband ample opportunity to extend himself. The evening was a success and the idea gleaned was to entertain no more than one couple at a time in our home. It worked.

Entertaining one couple was easy, informal, and enjoyable for both of us. Once the wheel started turning we occasionally dropped in on another couple or invited a couple to join us for a movie. Mini-scale sociability became less nerve-wracking all the way around and less a freeze-up for my husband.

Besides this, Lord, we agreed that incompatability in marriage is a lot of little things, decided to deal with this before it got beyond us, and we did.

*I wanted to help them but didn't know how.
Every fall the migrants swoop upon our community, pick the tomato crops clean, and dis-
appear into the night.*

THEY DON'T SPEAK ENGLISH, LORD, AND YOU KNOW I
don't speak Spanish. When they hit the county our citizens
put double locks on their doors and batten down the hatches
on community recreational facilities. Merchants sit up all
night and guard their cash registers for fear of theft.

Only children under eight and new mothers are excused
from field labor. Driving by their camp I saw flocks of
toddlers inside the wire fencing. I wondered whether the
community erected fences to keep the children safe or the
community safe. Facilities were substandard and mentally I
saw TEMPORARY stamped on everything—here today, gone
tomorrow.

Guilt and a little fury rippled through me. What could I
do, Lord?

I began with flowers as my international language. My
garden was not spacious but it was blooming profusely. I cut
enough for a small basket, drove to camp, and parked square
in the midst of the metal huts. This alone aroused curiosity.
Children gathered but not close. They hung back and a few
ran when I walked closer. It wasn't long before a young
woman appeared, nursing a baby as she walked. Perhaps she
was protecting the children from a stranger. Smiles were
exchanged and I handed her some flowers.

We said nothing. Another woman appeared and the same thing happened. In fifteen minutes the flowers were gone. I waved to all of them and got back to the car. A few waved meekly.

In two days I repeated the operation but included a red ball and a cardboard carton of wooden blocks gathered from scrap at the lumber yard. There was no hesitation when I tossed the ball to a little boy.

Helping the young mothers was harder. Then, Lord, I hit upon using those baby scales in my attic. With sign language and smiles I coaxed a mother to lay her baby on the scales. I wrote 10 on a paper and gave it to her. Another mother did the same and I wrote 11.2 on a paper. No other mothers appeared.

In five days I returned with another ball and large wooden beads for stringing. I carried the baby scales and eight young mothers appeared. I nearly cried with joy to see eight. Their babies were weighed, our sign language became enthusiastic, and Spanish filled the air as they compared weights of their babies. It was fun, even though I couldn't understand a word they said.

For six weeks I went out twice a week, sometimes to play with the children, always to weigh the babies. There were twelve women with babies less than two months old and a few women in waiting.

You know, Lord, at summer's end I left the scales and had traded a few English words for a few Spanish ones. Since then I have wondered a thousand times what happened to the people on that particular wave of the migrant stream.

WANTED:

One middle-aged saint
to sit 3 adorable children
while harried mother
goes back to work.
Salary Negotiable

*The ad was light enough to be attractive
and descriptive enough to be informative.*

STAYING HOME, LORD, WAS LIKE BEING HELD HOSTAGE
by three kids, a six-room house, and a station wagon. You
know I loved my family, but I sprang the trap between children and career to enlarge the shape of my human identity.

It had to be. I was getting schizophrenic at the stove and
felt I was shrinking into oblivion. The monotony of dailyness
choked me.

"Motherhood is so fulfilling," said my mother.

"Get a job," said my husband.

And I did. First, I threw out my survival kit of tran-

95

quilizers and aspirin. Next, I ran the ad and got eight replies
—one responded by mistake, two wanted the gold in my teeth
as salary, one should apply for army general, three were wash-
outs, and one was Mary Poppins who came by Chevy instead
of umbrella. Glee over her daily arrival made me leary on
whether I was being replaced at the starting gate before the
race.

Next, I gave full time to job hunting. By education I was
an English major, by training a typist, by dream a lady as-
tronaut, and by desire a cub reporter.

The *Daily Gazette* was no *New York Times* but it took me
on as assistant to the assistant to the assistant Woman's Editor.
I covered births, deaths, and Bar Mitzvahs. This meant little
desk time and a lot of road running.

"It's meant for me. Overnight the world is twice as big,"
I told my husband.

"Have you notified NASA? It's not as far to Mars as it used
to be," he joked.

Everyday I filled him in on local activities of the Elks, Lions,
Rotary, PTA, Cub Scouts, and Fireman's Auxillary—plus who
died or who had a baby.

Dinner conversation soared and the kids saw me as someone
other than a referee. Mother continued to see me as traitor.
I saw me as an intelligent human being highly in love with
life eager to stretch over the myriad of possibilities to create
my identity as a human being.

Lord, not every woman needs or wants time out for the care
and feeding of herself, but without it, for me, life was dis-
combobulated as visiting hours at the zoo.

96

I'm caught in cross fire between my son's nonviolence and his father's, "He's a draft dodger."

BEING A GO-BETWEEN MAKES HEADACHES, LORD, BE-cause it splits my loyalty. I have prayed harder, read more on the war, compared notes with other mothers, and listened for secondhand views about the draft board. I stand between a son whose life was being interrupted by circumstances beyond his control to fight a war he can not condone and a husband who marched to a different drummer when he donned a uniform in World War II.

I live on ifs—if he gets called, if he flunks out of college, if he takes off for Canada, if the draft board is rough, if he goes to war. Nothing is more unnerving, Lord, than being controlled by uncontrollable uncertainties.

I have felt I had to do something besides wait so I checked out opportunities for draft counseling. There were several nearby. One was in the high school, one in a college, and two were through clergymen. Somewhere I read that these centers were to provide information on rights and obligations under the present draft law and that was what I needed.

I have discovered that two views of patriotism in one family often causes cracks in the family wall and my role is to help avoid a chasm. At times I have been on guard duty twenty-four hours a day with danger from inside as great as from the outside.   It has been tempting to wring my hands, take aspirin, and dodge the issue by saying, "Well, that's life."

Above everything else, Lord, I have discovered that a go-between lives a dilemma and such a spot is literally for the stronghearted.

I'm out of excuses. It has to be today. The least I can do for those old people is to go out and visit. I'll do it this afternoon—tomorrow—next week. For years I have been the worst procrastinator when it comes to calling on the sick and elderly.

LIKE SCARLET O'HARA I COULD PUT OFF UNTIL TO-morrow anything I didn't want to do today. You knew that, Lord.

Our town is large enough to have several nursing homes and a fair-sized home for the aged. Much of the active club and church work finds expressive outlets in these places. Members call on the sick, remember them on birthdays, takes oldsters for rides, and almost adopt them as second mothers and fathers.

I drive and have a lovely home. It would have been easy for me to volunteer for service. Other women give programs, teach craft classes, read aloud, write letters, and entertain oldsters for meals.

I was the world's worst caller, but recognition of and guilt over the problem did not cure it. Lord, I was out of excuses and had disguised my procrastinations long enough.

Why?

My analysis began with honesty. I realized:

1. Old people depressed me. Their fears and pains rubbed off on me and I reacted with pity. They

99

were awkward and often spilled things. Some cried easily and shuffled around the halls looking pitiful. My sensitivity level is low and after making calls it would take hours to shake off my depression.

2. Some reminded me of my parents. This left me lonely. I would transplant myself into earlier years when Mother sewed my dresses and Dad would carry me on his shoulder saying, "Here's my girl!"

3. Involvement would mean getting too attached. When death came it would be like losing parents again and throw me into grief.

The solution took a combination of fact and courage.

1. If any of the oldsters had been my parents and I lived a distance away, it would be wonderful to know someone was taking them for a ride or inviting them to lunch.

2. Not all the oldsters were sick and weepy. Some were active as bear cubs and as lovable.

3. I wasn't moving in—only dropping in. Sitting through a game of Scrabble was such a little thing to do.

Lord, it has been two years since I worked through this problem and I still avoid becoming too attached. I enjoy making one or two weekly visits to assist friends on walks through the flower garden. (They love to be outside but have constant fears of falling.) My donated piano now sets in one of the living rooms. Playing it for group singing is much more fun than playing it at home by myself.

I hate the city and would move to the sub-urbs in a minute if my husband agreed. He says the city is where the action is, alive and kicking with excitement, theater, change, and opportunities. I see it alive and kicking with crime, strikes, poor schools, and noise. Our two teen-agers can't see any difference because school is school and the youth scene is one and the same.

LORD, YOU KNOW I WASN'T BORN WHERE COWS MOO and where wealth is judged by the acre of corn. I'm small city where neighbors take care of each other's goldfish during vacations and summer excitement is fireworks on the Fourth of July.

I'm not running from interracial neighbors or crime. To think so is sheer ignorance because the suburbs may be homogenized in five years.

I'm running to a slower-paced life with patio and green trees, Lord—where kids' voices are heard instead of mass transit every eight minutes.

When evening comes I'd like to smell the roses instead of car fumes and walk the dog in the grassy backyard.

"The suburban thing is dead, honey. Those guys spend half their time commuting to the city and the other half wishing they lived in here."

"Commuting is the only drawback. I'd like to trade the city for quietness, privacy, and healthier air."

"For two months you would but the first time a new gallery opened you'd head for the city. Or at midnight after a show you'd hate like the devil to ride twenty miles home instead of twenty minutes on the subway. In the suburb we'd have to get up at 6 A.M. for you to drive me to a seven o'clock commuting train. After that . . ."

"After that I'd go back to bed."

"Yeah, from exhaustion and boredom."

"No, she'd go out to smell the roses," my son joked.

"You're both wrong. I'd read more, shop more wisely, cook more, and stop griping about the city."

"I go for the part about more cooking," my son said.

"I go for the part about less city gripes," my husband said.

So it goes, Lord. Daily I read the real estate pages listing suburban property with woodland lots and swimming pools.

> . . . little garden 15′ wide, double garage, master bedroom opens on patio . . .

> . . . sliding glass doors open from living room into beautiful yard; large fireplace in study; carriage lamps line driveway . . .

Twice by appointment I looked at suburban property and resold the realtor on joys in the suburb. Another time we attended an office picnic held at a suburban home. I was hopeful it would sell my husband on a move, but some of the men griped about waiting an hour to tee off at the golf course and others couldn't golf at all because their yards were full-time operations. One woman decried the female neighborhood where men are absent from seven to seven, five days a week.

It is possible, Lord, that at my age I'm having an epidemic of restlessness and continuous flapping over this issue will do no more than antagonize the family.

The city pinches me, it is true. It is also true that I may be dreaming up another grass-is-greener fantasy, and if my husband would agree to move, I would run for the nearest escape hatch from the whole idea.

*At twenty-two I was a bride. At forty-two
I was a widow in shock with three children.
I wasn't smart enough to be a widow. Much
of the time I felt the bank cracking its whip
and tax authorities rattling brass knuckles
in a devious conspiracy to confuse me.*

AFTER TWO YEARS AS A WIDOW, LORD, I STILL FELT
like a tourist passing through but not belonging. In reflection,
I saw that marriage had taken the gamble out of living. In
widowhood risk became total. Jack didn't have a will and
our only piece of ownership was the house. I could not
drive the car or get into the safe deposit box without wading
through red tape. Until the great triumvirate of attorney-
banker-tax men snapped the tape I lived on the installment
plan. I felt like the Statue of Liberty with perpetually raised
hand asking permission from someone.

Financially, I consulted others but trusted no one. I felt
everyone was oggling my pocketbook. You know, Lord, that
ragged edges appeared on my personality and inner rebellion
rustled. At times I must have appeared mobilized for war-
fare. Since then, I have learned that severe irritability is a
natural symptom of deep grief. I became a person unreal to
me—suspicious of every repairman and every bill that arrived
for fear of being cheated.

The combination of grief and business ignorance is unbear-
able—as well as unpardonable. Wives have a way of saying,
"I'm not interested in business." "My husband takes care of

it." "I don't understand things like that."

Most of us, Lord, know little more than how to apply for a credit card. For me, that changed in a hurry. My grief took the course of overwhelming responsibility—at first overwhelmed by responsibility then overwhelmed with activity to conquer responsibility. In the next few months my emotions swung between total inability and total assurance. Wherever I hung on the scale I was tense and drained of energy. I lost the mental image of what my husband looked like. I felt intense guilt that my business decisions were not as he would have wanted. The happy past was consumed by the bewildering present. I couldn't pray, but it helped to believe that my husband was with me with gentle understanding.

Friends were gentle, too—maybe too gentle. Recently, I have wondered whether I required or deserved much loving kindness.

My most spectacular break in grief came unexpectedly when a friend urgently requested that I go with her to help another grief-stricken woman.

"I can't possibly help her."

"You're the only one among us who can because you've been through it."

"I'm a total stranger. How could that help?"

"By experience you're a soul sister. What difference if she doesn't know your name?"

I went, Lord, and only You knew what it took out of me and only You know what it gave me in return. All I did was give her space to cry, to talk, to spill her guilt, to wonder about the future, and to feel inadequate. In a few weeks I felt like a veteran home safe after having done battle on the front lines. The woman may never remember anything I said or did during my visits, Lord, but she realized someone else had passed that way and understood.

Other women pray over problems. I've tried but can't. Prayer, for me, is like playing blind man's bluff—a reach in the dark to touch someone you doubt is there.

LORD, YOU KNOW I BELONG AND AM ACTIVE IN A church. I believe in what we are doing and Sunday worship is meaningful. In fact, I need it. When our pastor leads prayer, I listen and pray with him. But when I'm alone, I can't pray.

Such feeling has triggered my guilt and I slammed the door on it for fear of being discovered. I intensified my reading on the subject of prayer, and chapters on "Why Pray?" and "Hindrances to Prayer" were helpful. Some books suggested short devotionals as preludes to prayer, but my mind hopped from subject to subject and the forced discipline nearly hypnotized me.

Asking the pastor about this would have been embarrassing and initiating it for discussion would have a dead giveaway.

Recently, when I was trying to meditate my son raced through the back door yelling, "Mom, you're not listening!" That was it! I knew it! It was true. I didn't believe anybody was listening when I prayed. It was as simple as that—and why keep on talking to Somebody who's not listening?

The problem was not prayer at all, Lord. It was and is my concept of You—whether You are personal, know me,

107

are interested in me, and listen to me when I talk with You. Now I've changed my reading topic, feel excited over my discovery, and not at all guilty.

Forgive me, Lord, for my tardiness to get You in focus.

I'm nobody special—just work in a travel office and belong to a church and bridge club. I live in an apartment with a school teacher. An opportunity to change jobs has left me floundering.

OPPORTUNITY CHARGED AND SNORTED, LORD, WHILE I paced the paddock making lists of pros and cons.

WHY CHANGE JOBS?
more open door for advancement
less pressure from the brass
more opportunity for creativity
more fulfilling
have status as a manager
WHY NOT CHANGE JOBS?
seems impractical
present security
forfeit 3-week vacation
forfeit easy routine
forfeit regular hours
requires more physical energy
small loss in salary
parental disapproval
no hospitalization
need a car

The lists became as wordy as the *Congressional Record* and as impersonal as the Kinsey Report, so I threw them out and headed for the starting post.

For eleven years I had worked in a travel bureau. It was not as glamorous as their posters but a good job. Designing vacations for others is a lot of nitty-gritty with criticism. Then on wings of luck an acquaintance was made manager of an International Traveler's Aid Center which included a gift shop of international crafts. She needed a manager. I took the job with little know-how and a heap of courage. Only You, Lord, know how much courage it took.

It meant study of import laws, frequent travel to buy, selection of personnel as salesmen, setting up artistic displays, and learning to appreciate the intricacies of the crafts and idiosyncrasies of the craftsmen.

"You buy?"

"Not yet. I'll look around."

"No cameo carving like it anywhere . . . is special . . . is delicate . . . is cheap . . ."

"It is beautiful and finely cut."

Proud of my ability to bargain I finally bought four. That night at the hotel I discovered a news article on cameo hucksters.

It was one of a dozen times I got taken.

Once I bought a few Canadian "original" wood carvings—Made in Japan.

Determination to excel vindicated my mistakes. So did an understanding boss.

First year profit was diluted by my ignorance. Costs were too high so I took a night course on How to Succeed in Business by Failing First. I made acquaintances and notes. It paid off. I had open house for club women and travelogue tours through the shop. Costumed friends did gift wrapping and high-school art students competed in our international window display contests.

Creatively I came alive, Lord. Only You know how one idea hatched another. Whenever a door opened for me to talk about native crafts or to be interviewed, I accepted. Two years before I would have crawled under the nearest rock.

Strangely enough, Lord, my self-image expanded as business expanded. I began to feel like a success. People listened when I spoke. Monetarily, I'm not far ahead of where I would have been on the other job, but psychologically I am rich with new acquaintances, wider opportunities for self-expression, more physical vitality, and happy commitment to my job.

The news depresses me. In the morning it makes me gloomy and at night it keeps me awake. Everything seems so mixed up that everytime it pours I think the Lord is pondering, "Forty days and forty nights and I could start over."

SO WHAT ELSE IS NEW?

If it's not a landslide in Tibet, Lord, it's a tornado in Kansas, a murder in London, or an air crash in Tokyo. We hear the news before the event is over. In color, every tragedy falls into the living room. Outside we get it via portable radio, and on every quiet Sunday outing, from a car radio. It's inescapable. There is no place to hide from the world.

Frequently, I would take a sabbatical from it and live in my vacuum pretending everything was resting in peace. Worst of all, Lord, I built a tough hide so events could roll off and not penetrate. This erased my sensitivity to the dangerous point of actually believing, "Whatever will be, will be."

No one cures the news. Tragedies, crimes, and catastrophes are here to stay. Today we learn the details faster and with commentary. Between Early Bird satellites and all-night radio stations, man has wired himself for sound.

Lord, I live in the world without permit to bury my head in the sand. Facing that fact shook me to my senses. I can't live here and render the world invisible.

Now I am juggling the alternatives of what this means to

113

my involvement at various points, Lord, but decisions come hard. When I decide to become actively involved, it won't be to build an ark. Maybe this time the world is worth saving.

WESTERN UNION

May 1

URGENT
To All Employees

We regret to announce as of July 1
Plant #7 will close operations.
Personnel will not be transferred
into other branches of the company.
Employees are requested to look
elsewhere for employment.

WE WERE ONE OF 702 FAMILIES WHO FOURTEEN
months ago received the telegram. The town rocked in disbelief. There had been no warning. Lord, You must have
been deluged with prayers that day.

My husband is fifty-four. Where does one go for employment, Lord, after twenty-seven years with one company? His
job was designing complicated, intricate equipment for weaving miles of fibers into fabric. In the entire plant only two
men were trained and equipped for this. "Shouldn't have
specialized, Millie. It's working against me," he kept repeat-
ing.

Within two weeks the housing market was flooded. A
town of ten thousand does not absorb quickly a real estate

deluge of seven hundred houses. We did not list our home but listed pros and cons on the entire situation.

In order to avoid a savings drain three of us got jobs while my husband mailed over sixty personal résumés of his career. He heard from less than fifteen. Most of these said he was too specialized or too old or they couldn't pay his salary level. Two asked for interviews. He flew to Georgia and Texas. Neither job panned out.

Our friends were having the same experiences although some did not own their homes, which raised additional urgencies. Everyone was full of endless rumors.

"The plant has been resold and will hire everybody."

"The plant is picking up the moving tab as compensation."

Presently, I am running a tight ship on family finances and balancing a full-time job as court house receptionist. Luckily, I found a job.

Worry wastes energy, Lord, but I can't control it. I keep telling myself I have the intelligence to deal with this emergency, but encouraging my husband and bucking up the kids is draining. John is considering part-time work, but I feel it would keep him from job hunting. At first the children and I assured him, "Dad, we'll hold the fort until you find something you want, not something you just settle for." Now we're at the point of urging settlement for anything.

Most of our close friends have moved. A few had lucky strikes on jobs. Others struck out to use parental homes as base.

My husband has given up hope of pay and social position equal to that which we have been accustomed. We pulled out of the country club and wrote letters of apology to the church and the United Fund for our unpaid pledges. Lord, we haven't lost our pride.

One of our blessings is family unity. We are pulling together, Lord. Dick is running the elevator at the bank and Janice is working at the library. Our savings have not been touched. Last week John was offered a job in the newspaper circulation department. Salary is half what he has had but it means staying in our home. Whether or not he takes the offer is his decision, but please, Lord, help him think it through.

My decision is to do everything within me to be strong spiritually and maintain the philosophy that if problems are essential to growth I have a great opportunity. Each day, Lord, I count my blessings of health, a comfortable home, and a wonderful family. I blame no one—not the plant manager, not bad luck, not You. Economic circumstances altered our future and thankfully we haven't bounced beyond recovery but are simply backtracking and starting again. Life is still a precious package, Lord, although we have shed all illusions about its ease.

Life is a rat race and I'm losing I have so much on my mind it makes me shake my wheels are turning twenty-four hours a day if I'm not straining over mental lists I'm cramming in something today which should have been done yesterday.

LORD I USED TO SIT DOWN AND LUMP EVERYTHING together but I've stopped because futility sets in now I can't even sit down I have so much to do this is my second family I have a married son with four kids in three different schools I belong to three Parent-Teacher groups two Girl Scout troops Cub Scouts and the Babe Ruth League this makes a lot of hauling hollering mending picking up socks and patting on Band-Aids sometimes without thinking I forget the neighbors last names because I know them best by their kids dogs turtles and two-wheelers everybody tells me to calm down and drop outside activities but good mothers pitch themselves into the fray maybe I have too many kids for my age but it's too late to return any I'm forever experimenting on efficiency and some of it helps for instance it's easier to take four to the dentist on one trip once I got so efficient I misplaced the tea-kettle and traced it to the refrigerator where efficiently I had shelved it with Jello assigning jobs helps but I'm restless until they're completed making lists helps if I remember to nail down the list so it doesn't become a resting place for bubble gum my best help is when I don't cram in more than one problem at a time problems are the only thing I handle one at a time everything else comes cheaper by the dozen or with coupons I figure Lord in fifteen more years I've got it made at least that was my plan until yesterday when my five year old said Mommy when I get big I want lots of babies and we'll live here and eat peanut butter and jelly.